CRADLES

NOMADIC
PRESS

OAKLAND WORKSPACE

2926 FOOTHILL BOULEVARD #1
OAKLAND, CA 94601

BROOKLYN WORKSPACE

475 KENT AVENUE #302
BROOKLYN, NY 11249

WWW.NOMADICPRESS.ORG

MASTHEAD

FOUNDING AND MANAGING EDITOR
J. K. FOWLER

ASSOCIATE EDITOR
MICHAELA MULLIN

DESIGN
BRITTA FITHIAN-ZURN

MISSION STATEMENT

Nomadic Press is a 501 (C)(3) not-for-profit organisation
that supports the works of emerging and established
writers and artists. Through publications (including
translations) and performances, Nomadic Press aims
to build community among artists and across disciplines.

SUBMISSIONS

Nomadic Press wholeheartedly accepts unsolicited
book manuscripts, as well as pieces for our annual
Nomadic Journal. To submit your work, please visit:
www.nomadicpress.org/submissions

DISTRIBUTION

Orders by trade bookstores and wholesalers:
please contact Small Press Distribution,
1341 Seventh Street, Berkeley, CA 94701
spd@spdbooks.org
(510) 524-1668 / (800) 869-7553 (Toll Free)

This book was made possible by a loving community of family and friends, old and new.

For author questions or to book a reading at your bookstore, university/school,
or alternative establishment, please send an email to info@nomadicpress.org.

Cover Art by Grace Millard (www.gracemillard.com)

Published by Nomadic Press, 2926 Foothill Boulevard, Oakland, California, 94601

First printing, 2017

Printed in the United States of America

Library of Congress Cataloging-in-Publication Data

Cradles
p. cm.
Summary: Obsessed with hunger and the mythology of safety,
the poems in *Cradles* interrogate violence, desire, and nativity
along lines of both the angelic and the everyday.

[1. Poetry. 2. Selections.] I. III. Title.

2017916437

ISBN 978-0-9981348-7-1

CRADLES

FISAYO ADEYEYE

NOMADIC
PRESS

To my brother and sister

CONTENTS

THOMAS, THE DOUBTER

CROWN SHYNESS

KINGDOMS

BLACKFISH

IN THE BEGINNING

ACKNOWLEDGMENTS

SHOUT OUTS

THOMAS, THE DOUBTER

Flail

A god eating his boy on the banks.
This is a dream: the lamb gutted

and hung, smoke-stained.
The braided strand of hair hanging

down his mother's cheek.
The very word hung pulled over

heat as the body burns,
skin around muscles soft,

still hardening. Splitting
and blackening under the hot mouth

of the flame. In the night,
the pup pushing through the plastic,

feather-mouthed: coughing
and pink. In the morning,

the calcified remains
already gone. Stripped

skin to ghost.

Portrait of Wrecks

She carried the body like a painting.
And when done, pushed the color out.

See the portrait now. Glass cracking
into lines of red. A mouth painted without color.

A brush of fur and wool scraping the last
hue from the shell. His mother cuts

a switch from the tree. First a branch, now a limb.
Pulls all the tiny splinters from her fingers

with a pair of cold metal tweezers.

Imagine Boy made both flinch and blush. A dark
color clinging to the top of the water thick.

See the portrait now. The breaded fish tongue
glowing over the hot pot. Roasted almonds.

Warm sweat pooled in a clean cup.
The cup lifted to her lips.

Long Island

To have and to hold,
like a body wrapped around a bullet:
a peach wrapped around a peach pit.

They say a man is in there, cutting a grave
into the bed. He says, *welcome
to the city. It's all Bridges and Cradles*

from here. We hide russet tree rings
under our tongues, so he can't see how old
we aren't. We hang paper lanterns

from the branches with kites and string.
Walking down the windy street,
we wonder where saints have gone.

If there are any left. If they are coming back.
We wonder how to explain our wrists,
our unfeathered faces. How to talk

about ourselves. You say, this is the body,
it is all meat. This is an answer, since
you keep asking for one: a man

is sitting out on the front porch
with a gun. He says he is waiting
for the angels to come.

Attestation

To be brief, there were fruit stems, dried.
Shredded wings. A body to salt the earth.
His father   shearing the lamb's fur
and spreading it over his broad shoulders,

tall grass cut down to his hips. I held out
the blade, as if to say you cannot predict
its future. But you can always predict.
It will do what it was made to do, *if*

indeed it was made. Nobody said it was me,
and never needed. I was always the dog,
the metaphor in the mouth of the gun that
didn't fire, but wanted so badly for a tiny

finger to hold it tight. Collapse as body
forgetting one word   then the next,
then the next. Collapse as body decaying.
Do you still think a wound is the only proof

you will ever need? Boy's cheek scrapes
bark and bullet shells fly past his face. He can
never be sure what doesn't kill him is not
still trying. But knows if he looks deep enough

into the barrel, he can almost see the anything
in anything.

Coals

Always some new object to pull from the ashes.
Two braids, two shivers tied together

in the same pod, and the black mouth
of the flame still pushing one crisp finger

back inside itself. *How else do you
come upon a voice?* His hands hovering

over my weak bones. A pair of objects
with nothing better to do, but still perhaps,

two things they should not be. Let's not talk
not talking. Let's talk about three voices

in the fire, unweaving the smoke into sound.
How every time Boy came back to me,

he had a new voice inside, spilling
from his lips. Black tongue and black teeth.

Everything stained ash from heat. A cigarette
in a burning bush. Boy in burning flesh.

His dry tongue cracking like bread.
Both spines etched into the back fence.

Evenings

He could paint a portrait from this,
the marriage of their bodies together,
the dance of the drowning. They will write

songs about this. The bride of Christ.
The water a dress. Ocean-jawed: wide
as anything. An apology she never needed.

His shirt gapes. His hips open and
her stiff fingers pull at peach fuzz
from beneath his boxers. They burn and

wet, burn longer. Boy stares at the color,
knows better than to eat another god's fruit.

Another garden. Another snake. Another prayer
stretching taut skin. Another hip
as foothold. Another shoulder blade

as place for leverage. Another river
breaking through. It always does.

When the Body Footnotes Birth

A bucket of crabs
spills over the sidewalk, and Boy

watches them scramble weakly
away. He is up in the morning,

trying to wash the smoke
from his mother's hair. White picket

teeth fencing in her face. Her throat
wrapped in water, and breath vanishing

in bubbling clouds. When you try
to stop yourself from breathing

by breathing. And it's not worth it.
And it never is. Crab fat

and white grease. Thin shells
drowning in a large pot,

the crustaceans chewed
into the green glass.

A body that wants to swallow,
the way every ocean does.

No More Metaphors

He said he had a dream her hand
was invisible under the water. The water

was clear. He knew it was over and she knew
it was over, the sea was just for show.

He walked slowly, carefully. As if the floor
was made of paper. Adam's ankles, Achilles'

apple, ribs of glass. There were no more metaphors
for the weakness of men. He knelt in the waves,

fed himself to the water one limb at a time
and watched the light quiver. He bent

and took tender sips of the foam. There were
no more metaphors for the violence of men.

CROWN SHYNESS

You Can Call It a Dream

if you want   If it makes you feel better
to peel paint off the walls   gently lower
pieces into your mouth   A rainbow
smiles in the oil slick   on the driveway
kids   play eviction   In summer
the damp bills melted   on our chests
mango peppered   made our lips   bleed
red   When you told me how this
could feel   my Big Gulp full   of bullets
your tongue wet   against cigarette paper
I twisted in pleasure   the front of my chest
turned   every possible color   It was
always so hard to sleep in the city   I never
knew what it meant if I didn't tremble   you
didn't tremble   If neither of us   trembled

When There Is Nothing, When

everything is gone   the difference between
breaking ground   breaking in   is the sound
You say,   you and I   are in a black and
white film   Our bones as light   as clear
as air   You held a bottle of nail polish
between your toes   gently applied, as I read
a story about saints   One body dragged
by horses   One body burned alive,
torn by lions   One eye gasping open
wet   You picked a new bottle
of polish   and painted my teeth
the tip of my tongue   brightred

We Learned to Discredit
   the Patterns

The way the world swallows   The way
babies sometimes sleep   with their
tiny fists clenched   Stuffed animals
& mashed potatoes   Bees eating
honey   from the inside   Nursing
at the flames   I was trying to hold
you without shaking   When you took
off your jacket   & laid it
like a bridge   across the water   I bent
pressing my lips   to my reflection
Not thirsty   But no longer wanting to burn

We Never Knew How to Speak
About the Rupture of a Body

without opening ourselves   but while
we were dying   we nibbled at fruit
looked at mirrors   We saw pretty things
sometimes   Chasing our whole lives
the feeling   of martyrdom   or satisfaction
the way   the past won't let you leave things
unless you love those things   I am trying
so hard to love you   so much more than
all these things   Take your tongue out
Take it   all the way out   lick then
swallow   the bruise mouth rim   Tonight
you're itching in places   you have forgotten
but you still have this whole life   You don't
have to go back   if you don't want to leave

Silver Pool

If the hand bloats after being bitten. If the match

is too wet to spark. If once touched, twice recoil,

if one knuckle, two knuckles, three knuckles. Four.

If it is December or September—

and the warm bread unfolds into your mouth.

If it is August or October—

and you hold a piece of ice on your tongue

then watch dead insects halo across the water.

If after five knuckles, six knuckles. Seven.

You shell the nut, study the navel, suck the candy

from its wrapper, and spit it back into my mouth.

If it is March or April, and your body finally catches

its ghost. If it is March or April, and your body

still doesn't know what to do.

Soft Rot

In summer, all of our dreams are wet.
I have fruit laying on a rooftop, staring
at the half-scooped moon, edges jagged

from the places you'd bitten into,
your teeth gleaming with the seeds.
Light splitting you in half.

If there is no entrance, you
create one. I looked for you in a flower patch.
Stuck two fingers in your mouth,

spread and listened, carefully.
You spoke meal. You spoke eat me,
then licked the spoon clean. Spit bubbling

the corners of your mouth, glittering
like fish larvae. I am trying not to look
at their little eyes. Just touch

to feel the color release from its source,
spread itself over my palm. We carve
the wings off our backs

and wring moisture from them. Our necks twist
at the same time. I can't remember when
rain ever felt this good. Like midnight

in warm mountains. Or slow sex
in a blue room.

Zugunruhe

Not the butterflies skirting the invisible
mountain. Just the quiet of nature as it

comes to witness murder. The dry insects
tracing human shapes in the carpet, though

the bodies are no more. How I have come
to witness these bodies. Paint their clean bones,

stipple their fresh rinds. Oil the lines in their
feathers. Wiping the light off my fingers,

I pull stroke after stroke to listen for a perfect
sound. Try to hear red. To live in it.

But every time it dries, it looks different
My father's gloss, my mother's scattered

spackle. The peaks and cliffs of old paint
buried beneath new.

Wash

We wait till the lake freezes over,
run across the surface.

You show me fish frozen under the ice,
tell me how they'll swim again, once it melts.

You say an animal who defines itself
in struggle is a good animal.

The washer breaks and our floorboards
sink under the water. We walk across

them barefoot, the green swimming thin
between our toes. On screen,

a grizzly bear dives and the glass rattles
from the static. And it reminds me of something

I once learned in therapy. If your relationships
with people are a symbol of how you feel

about a higher power.
If you can trust a body of water

no longer moving. Last week my therapist
pulled a long piece of blue thread

from his pocket and told me of a new type
of therapy. He pushed the thread through me

and I scanned the pelts and heads lined
across his walls, and knew

how he would mount me.

Loose Topography

I'm praying the empty
Goatsuckers shaken
my dry knuckles, tight
I'm praying black ants
I'm praying the hive's
of the swarm.
on the banks,
I'm praying
between the doors
I'm praying the death
around tiny bits of glass
the banks, the mud,
on my tongue, clear

red fields, in the heat,
from their feathers
from tightening.
humming the throat
geometric. I'm praying
The cocoons
the wet coils crawling
the yellow noose of
gentle vibrations
trap music. I'm praying
broken eggshells.
the wings of flies.
like water

a boxful of birds
and I am praying in
The fence, the grass
of the golden oak
the chaotic spread
shaking
toward the surface
spider silk hanging
along its thread
the worms crawling
I'm praying
The oil dissolving
and insect blood.

March Elegy

My brother holds vigil gently, as though
it might break. Ghosts don't read vacate

notices, don't mind a room's dirt. Cockroaches
crawl through the wet lips of overturned bottles.

Our eyes pan over meat spoiled with maggots
and squint till our screens fill with war. In battle

we ate on our knees. Sometimes, standing up.
Sometimes, running. When the water was poisoned,

we drank air. When air was poisoned, we went back
to water. In times of peace, we watched stars fall

against the dark liquid. Thought them reflections. Two years
from now, this exact spot, tree trunks will be swallowed

by black ice. God shivering earthquakes in the snow.

The queen pumps wet and white
into the dying grass.

A panic that smells
like exodus, but always
looks like panic.

Everything teems
in small gray beads
around an aching root.

The trees won't budge,
the cells no longer scream

when they separate.

The boys eat blind
and slow
around their tender bodies.

Their new kingdoms:
real, their   old kingdoms:

dream.

KINGDOMS

Deer Territory

Bury us where
the neighborhood begins.

Under the bridge, his neck curves
into something architectural,

I pocket green hip bones, tracing
the freckled spots for luck, or maybe

something alphabetic: red ants
swarming meat and sinew, baby fat,

crumbs chewed into the tips of
our fingers: Divine.

As we bike the long, winding road
spilling past our cul de sac,

bare trees and tiny feathered
bodies toss the landscape.

No angels, we think.

But angels here.

Inland

the block remembered each boy / she had pushed screaming / into the light / but sometimes she forgot / the hang of their clothes / the shape / of their spines / pushing back / against the cotton / our father spread anointing oil / on our foreheads / before school and we walked / around all day / with his fingerprints on our faces / flickering down towards / our mouths / sweetness and / salt / after we were cloned / we felt the many parts breathe / expand inside of us / we pressed / a tongue back and the animal snapped like / it was bred to be / remember / the sound our bodies made / as we moved in channels through / one another / *burnt sugar* / *babies bandaged after birth* / we knew the block had seen / a million bodies / just like / ours

Genesis

Found mid-shift and shuddering   over dry scales.
It begins with hunger,   as it does always.   The muffled
clicks of mouth bones disconnecting.   The blue sap

gathering in its throat.   Eyes glaze and shadow   like clouds
pooling over a filmy lake.   It tries something like speech
and cries off   voice torn 'round a forked tongue

that flicks and spreads smaller tongues,   petals, fingers.
Congealed skin oiled between new knuckles.   Hard to change,

harder still to keep.   The body blinks.   Corpse
colored eyes browning in sunlight.   Pulls a tongue briefly
to catch the edge of dead skin   floating in the breeze.

Afterglow

|

I remove our line and so / I remove our distance / Tell me the thing you did / after washing the walls / after painting the tree branch / through the kitchen window / with your eyes / You corrected the blue / by coughing / bits of color hung in the corners / in the limits / I was so thirsty I tried to chew the water / as it passed in / disoriented / a gasp of wet cloth / caught between my thighs / a block of soft wax / caramelizing / the chrysalis I had spun / in my sleep

||

The neighbor's son hugs his bones / instead of eating / He breathes through / a mask made of paper / a circle spreading / Death in every shape / If you press into him / You might feel at first / his taut skin / in the empty space / Curl your fingers / in his locks / and you might find how heavy / the heat he leaves / The door is open / his fingernails floating in / the sink / The red plastic melting / in the sun / Everything in his mouth / tastes sweet / and sour / all at once

Passed Over

Though I walk through the valley of the shadow,

though I walk as shadow, though I linger in death,

I will be brief. Mary did you know how your child's

mouth would become an offering? How good

it would look in an open-lipped gape on a plate of gold?

Take the boy from the field. Take him anywhere

his dry hair won't break like wheat. Look at your child

now, pressing his lips into each cut of cold steel,

carrying a cross into his room and dragging

it onto the bed, fingerprint bruises in his arms. How

fiercely he holds your love against his chest.

How gently he holds your love against love.

Crucifixion
after M.K. Foster

Blessed be that Nazarene. Blessed be the Nazarene's thin-whipped arms spread eagle on split wood. Blessed be that split wood, yellow emergency tape and pegs that spread holes in the palm like the bruised lips of an apple-rose. Blessed be the boy dreaming the bullets they fired into his mother's house, the tightened knots in the rope they hung over the tree. Blessed be the boy pulling himself from the wood, wiping the rain from his forehead, scooping the reddened sweat out of his collarbones. Blessed be how Nazarene lays his back against the surface. The way the dirt smokes underneath like fog. Blessed be that fog, those precious minutes between *oh no*—a dirty mouthful of lake water. How Nazarene ran with his t-shirt balled and bloody, and tossed it before doubling back, raking his fingers through the surface to claim it again, fishing lines whistling sharp over his head, lips so fat a hook could get caught in them. Blessed be the hooks still caught in them. Blessed be how the Nazarene ran and when the men finally caught him, whipped him, until he swore he saw angels unpeeling their wet wings from the trees. Blessed be the way that Nazarene bit the bullet, broke his teeth, let himself spread across the lake. Blessed be the way he tilted his head to see a gray sky scarred by birds.

CCD

My sister lifts herself from the pool,
wet braid a black snake curled
around her neck. Me and my brother
flip playing cards on the roof,

a neighborhood you might know.
The porch made soft from termites,
sinking under our sneakers.
The spider webs revealed by morning dew.

We don't run in the house. We don't leave
our shoes on the carpet. We hide in the garden,
hold the red bulbs high. Shiver as we drink.
Our parents never notice the sunken eyes,

the transparent wings shriveled to our hips,
bones protruding against our stomachs.
How late August, white pollen always catches
in the dips of our hoodies. How the guns

always sound like cars backfiring.

Empire

Sundays in Loma Linda
    were sun-warmed grapes, half priced

        menthols. Books swollen with rain
         water left on sides of the road.

            When you turned on the air, you could
          almost smell the ocean. See how edges
         become more fragile than middles.

Every morning, I pulled the dry film from
    my lips. Today, we bought bottles
        of warm water and visited our old houses.

           In the Northeast: the bees hummed
               until the glass cooled.

    Southwest: the gas smelled sweet
when it was left on.

           Northwest: caught between the mesh
           and the window,

    I once flung my body into the glass
        again and again, for the moon.

Thread with Unwaxed String

and the bow bends. This is what happens
after and it never stops. We burnt the things

clinging to the sides of our pockets.
I burnt the look you tossed me

across the classroom, our teacher flashing slides
of bodies hanging from trees. That night

I burnt quietly, repeatedly, in my bed.
I could never find words for

the feeling of needing my nose cracked.
My scent, smothered. Overwhelming desire

to be calved.   Spawned,
                                          spread.

Over summer, there was never need
to worry. Our mother would give birth

with the bedroom door open.
Hanging limp off the edge

of a steel bedframe, insect eggs
quivering gingerly

between her leg hairs.

more light // more mouths to feed

The cicadas scream // until their shells crack.
I push Polaroids

under the water and the liquid bends
our mouths into clean black lines.

What is a day if you're not worried
about survival?

Three people died in the city this morning

sitting on a bench
staring into the cloudy sky, watching a bird
drawn into a draft //

wing jerking // how ungraceful it looked. How strange

it felt to have witnessed it.
Like watching God slip

His finger through the small bullet mouths //
Sucking holes into their t-shirts

as if searching them // for sound.
Or maybe, just proof

Murmuration

A type of learned affection in the swarm.   All that heat.
A beetle trapped on its blue back   struggling with the stiff
mandibles of ants.   Spine unbroken, belly soft.   Pulled
out of.   Doesn't scream   just spreads its jaws
again   and again.   When the shell finally
cracks, it sounds like a train   bending. Some
color pouring down its legs.   Wide chest spilling
like cool milk. White plumage   spreading over new bones.
Breathes 'til tiny spots speckle   the ends
of its beard. Breathes   again and again.

BLACKFISH

White Whale

We have soft spots for ugly fruit, but the outline
in the fruit patch is human shaped. Boy sleeps

lightly powdered, a sweet mouth, ants crawling
through his tangled locks. When he awakes, he feels

half-drowned, like the Osprey in the river. The one
that wanted something bright pulled from the back

of its throat. A dark intimacy: these bird feathers and
blood stains smeared over his bedsheets, these fingers

slick with juice. Police said Boy caught a bullet like he
was reaching for it. But these days Boy rises

and Boy rises again.

Lazarus

Turning her hands over in the flour, her palms are
twin doves, unwrung necks. Boy pushes his body

through the breadcrumbs, cinnamon salt. Pushes
one dry white thumb straight into the middle

of his chest, until the seed dips into his heart.
Candied walnut. He licks the wet sugar from his

fingers before they dry. Fruit peeled by fingernail
or by knife: same song in the same skin. Asleep in

the oven, his mother turns the heat low, scrapes
all the ash from the bottom. A panful of burnt

blue moths.

Breach

after Janine Joseph

An animal that knows the hunter by its bait
or animal that knows to bare its teeth

never the soft of its stomach. A boy drags a bad
body full of blood and his mother runs. Her boy-

pup thrown. Animal who runs for hours and hours
through dirty snow. Animal that smothers

its own ribbed muscle in mud and foliage. A
boy who knows a hunter by the bait, handcuffs

brushing his wrists sore. A slow dream.

A Country with No Windows

Chalk residue of flower petals on his fingertips,
Boy leaves the light on and remembers the leaving.

Reaching for the bent letter on the table, Boy pushes
his shoulders back. Wall sweating like a greenhouse,

a rabbit corpse drying in a cardboard box. There is
another angel gunned down in the driveway but

father closes the windows and wipes the gun
clean. Waking in the bathtub, Boy nearly breaks

his back trying to lift the body out. Pearl teeth
sore. The bath water stained tattoo blue.

Betrayal

Before their lips touched nothing happened.
After their lips touched nothing happened.

Nothing ever happened. Jesus nails Boy
to the cross, halo burning into his skull.

Catch your breath and give it back to me.
Anatomy of their bedroom: Flies hover

over fruit peels in the trashcan. Light blooms
and fades at the same time. The rain cut

the sky into so many pieces. There was
no more barking in the night. Boy says,

teach me to pray without bleeding. And
Jesus smiles, touches Boy's wet cheek.

Fever

Boy and Jesus on the bottom of the boat,
stale fruit-tin smell, elementary school

lunch stomachs. Jesus guts a fish and
throws it back. *You only throw live ones*

back, Boy says. You're doing it wrong.
They both burn dry ginger red. Smoke

cream from the apple cores. Boy never asks
what it feels like to want the wrong things in

the right ways. But some nights,
watches Jesus sit on top of the barn,

combing dark blood out of his hair.

Regicide

Boy and Jesus standing on the overpass.
Jesus points to where the street bends

until his eye forgets how to bend it.
He says his father died yesterday

on that corner. He died in his sleep like
an old man or an infant. Like branches

breaking in a breeze. He died like a king,
on his back. He died like a king, belly full.

He died like a king, his great head fallen
between his knees, dark hair sewn

into his scalp. Dressed and heathered
in the long road, Boy holds his hand

and for a long time, just holds.

Mainsail

Boy pulls himself up the wet cement,
unpeels and unpeels. Mother bakes

a pie in the morning. Dirty eyes, Swiss
hot chocolate. Remember how Boy

lost his baby teeth? Remember how
he picked the stars out of the sky one

by one? An hour in and he's still
there waiting. Boy pulls his hands back,

drags his shoulder lower. It will
always feel wrong, anyone's hands

on his face, pushing his mouth closed,
his stomach wet. The white moon gone.

Hunted

It feels like another survival, Boy's mouth
soft around pieces of breadfruit. Machete

sound cutting into the branches in the trees
outside the school. In ten years there will be

no way to catalogue this feeling, but
for now there are still those bent bridges,

those phantom bird calls through
Neighborhood Park. Boy drops a half-eaten

orange and it feels like an answer or a
signal: a pair of yellow eyes pace him in

the dark. Boy stifles a scream by pushing a
whole fist inside his mouth.

Blackfish

The sun spills a billion pale bodies loose
all at once. Boy watches the giant fish swim

against the tank towards him, pushes
the blue feeling up the front of his chest

until it shudders over. Weather: just his
body turning. Mouths: just choirs on

a bridge. Boy knows he's gone too far when
he loses horizon. The way his God will

plant bones and dream pink fields of men,
plant war and dream oceans overflowing.

Boy sits on a clean stone with lips carved
in red coral, his breath rings wet

like a dirty sea.

Emetic

Mother says having children is like painting
in reverse. First you have all these possibilities,

then you're essentially left where you began.
She keeps a small bowl by the bed to catch

the blood. Paint at the corner of her eyes. White
lips. Boy bites into the fruit and tastes the metal.

The power goes right out of his lungs. Dreams
where the sailboats are coming back. A gray color

exhaling. On the second day, Boy closes his eyes.
On the third day, Boy rises and Boy rises again.

Knots

Call him Ishmael. Tell him a black body is not
a white whale, and see if he believes you.

You can neglect this one until it grows. Chinese
Evergreen. Pothos on the roof. How the Boy spit out

all the coins he swallowed, so the boatman
wouldn't get them. Tell him it's the busman here.

Tell him your phones won't work, this far into
the field. How over there in the burnt succulent

patch, a black man sat and drank water until
he died, clawed fingers hooked in his too-thin bird

chest. Tell him a black body is not a white whale.
Tell him. And see if he believes you.

Surrender

Boy thinks a thing that he wants and
sometimes it appears. Every day

Boy gets up to fight God. He gets up
to go out into the world. Boy knows

he only felt like giving up when the lights
came back on. When he and God were just

small children on a bridge. When their
hands forgot the shapes hands could make

underneath all the red lights.
He thinks a thing he wants is to die

under a bridge. Watching that beached ship
bleeding that new gold ichor.

In the Beginning

|

there was the van they packed and the truck. Four times, both
ways. First Eden and then Neighborhood Park. A quiet city with no
fireworks allowed on the Fourth, no lights on after ten in the valley.

Just a man cutting a throat into the trunk

of a white oak tree in the front yard. Enclosed cavity echoing.

Afterwards, his mother took him out. Told him to bend a lily and
petals of lavender around one finger. Press it into the corners, *the
wounds.* Drag it across and write his name.

On Sunday, he stared at his hands,

fingers still chalky, while their pastor told the story of the beginning.
Their pastor said, in the beginning, there was a disease.

This disease existed everywhere. In everything. Until one day,

God couldn't take it, and opened Her mouth.

II

In the story of the beginning, Eve bit the fruit. She bit into the
soft of her cheek. Peeled back the yellow flesh, and passed pieces to
Adam. On the second day, Adam offered her his wrist.

On the third day, Adam offered her his throat.

On the first day, God came down, and pushed Her fingers into
Adam's stomach. Adam moaned

as She pulled out a honey-colored bone.

III

In his biology class, a giant bone sculpture

of a whale, carefully constructed. Hung.

The boy sitting next to Adam split the stomach of a frog, and asked
Adam what kind of animal he would want to be. Adam pretended
not to notice the boy didn't ask anyone else.

He drew a picture of this animal, and thought the painful swelling

of a beast's stomach too far into its meal. He thought the sound of
sating hunger. How the wind whistles behind a door

trying to catch the door.

On the second day, Adam and Eve named all the animals. *Honeybee.*
White throated sparrow. Fear. Desire.

IV

On nights like these, Adam's body felt like a bruised balloon.
His bedroom, an altar.

His bedroom, dark and full of hands.

In this story, Adam's body is trying to explain *body*, but can't,

and so quivers.

V

Sometimes Adam thinks lines of white lightning crossing over the
top

of the aquamarine sea. Sometimes, he thinks white veins spreading
through his arms like strings unraveling into light.

Sometimes he thinks, a bonfire in a bedroom

then a bedroom.

VI

On the third day, Adam meets Jesus, a towheaded boy

with a tank full of gas, a pair of hard headlights.

He had seen him before at school, but was always too shy to talk.

Jesus with his water bottles, and blue sneakers. With his striped
sweaters,
and plastic crosses.

He often wondered when Jesus sank under the water,

if the liquid would unpeel. Wondered if Jesus pulled his fingers
slowly
through the nerves at the back of Adam's neck,

if he would feel the bright pinches. If he would even know

that it hurt. On the fourth day, Adam carried himself slowly,
as though fully submerged.

VII

On the fifth day,

Adam watched the road men peeling the hot flesh from the
pavement in front of their new house, and daydreamed a buzzer

whispering gently

at the nape of his neck.

His mother hung wires and put in new curtains. She called this
dressing the house. She called this covering. Sheltering.

Adam had another dream: a body-shaped hollow cut into the tree,

his own body snug inside of it.

VIII

On the sixth day, a lizard dragged its belly across the hot sidewalk,
skin hanging from its back like a clear cape.

Adam's tongue pushed at the pieces of ash caught in his teeth.

Dirty wet oven. Dirty memory. Dirty fingerprint

on the cracked screen of his phone.

IX

Tuesday. Adam was never any good at sports,

but he tried.

Often, Adam noticed the other boys on the court looking him over,
like they were wondering what kind of animal he was.

Adam sometimes whispered *Deer*. Whispered softer. *Fear & Hunger*.

Out loud, he always said nothing. He ran down the street, near

the overpass. Only stopping at a field of red grass swaying.

He saw a dead bird tunneled out, being consumed by insects. A
bleached skull peeking through its torn brown feathers.

X

On the sixth day, Adam and Eve named all the plants.

Earthworms hung thick from the dirt and they pushed them back in

with their sneakers. They rubbed at the powder with the palms of
their hands. Dry skin peeling like snake scales.

After service, Adam and Jesus snuck into Jesus' father's study. The
afternoon sun coming in sticky and hot through the blinds. They
pulled the curtains closed, but it was still so hot in the room

that the skin of their thighs stuck together. So hot

they had to unpeel themselves from every hard surface.

XI

On the seventh day, God opened Her mouth and drowned

the world in birds.

XII

On the seventh day, Jesus gave Adam

a drink from his water bottle, and Adam's throat burned.

His mouth hanging open like a door, like a creature, waiting to be
welcomed inside, Adam stared

at the pink pinch of skin between his teeth. He imagined before he
bit, that the skin would move into the spaces his teeth would go.

XIII

On the seventh day, Adam and Eve snuck into the neighborhood
park.

Eve got her jeans caught in the teeth of the fence, and a line of red
dotted

her thigh. Adam untangled her and they ran
through the grass. The burning field,

Christmas lights choking all the trees.

XIV

Under the slide at the children's playground, Eve cracked her
knuckles against his chest.

And Adam smiled wide until his face split in half

then halved again. Wet seeds clinging on his chin, some
follow the line of cold sweat down his collarbones. A long river

coming between two small hills.

XV

Eve kissed Adam until he said *stop*. Eve kissed Adam until he said
nothing. Eve opened his chest, blew

his heart out like a flame, or a dandelion

spreading its head. Eve said she didn't need to know what kind of
animal Adam was. Only what kind of animal he sounded like.

Her mouth moist. Both their tongues tied

in thin ropes of spit.

XVI

The night loud with the sound of sirens. The morning

red with the sound of flight. The afternoon quiet

with the bodies of birds covering lawns, or being picked from the
pool water with leaf rakes.

In the morning, Adam thought about roadkill. Thought about
pulling pearl moons from an animal's throat. A stomach full of
broken clocks. The endless hunger of time and more time.

XVII

On the seventh day, rain fell in slow motion when it caught in the
light.

XVIII

On the seventh day, everything lasted forever.

Acknowledgements

Very grateful to the editors of the publications which the following poems (some in different forms) first appeared:

Rogue Agent: "Portrait of Wrecks"

Inferior Planets: "You Can Call It a Dream"

Vinyl: "Silver Pool"

VelRo Reader: "Loose Topography," "more light // more mouths to feed"

The Collapsar: "Fever"

The Wildness: "Inland"

Gap Tooth: "Wash"

Print Oriented Bastards: "Deer Kingdom"

Nailed Magazine: "Flail," "Attestation," "Evenings," "Passed Over"

NOTES:

"Passed Over" borrows language from Psalm 23:4 and "Mary, Did You Know?" as written by Mark Lowry and Buddy Greene.

Shout Outs

I cannot even begin to express my immense immense appreciation to all the amazing people who have encouraged me, spoke into me, believed in me, and inspired me. So in a feeble attempt to catalogue some of the many I have felt influenced by throughout the journey of creating this book:

Want to give love again to Lolade and Victor, my amazing sister and brother, who are two of the most creative and generous people I know. To my parents for dealing with me and my siblings and working hard to give us the best life possible.

Want to give love to the Imagining the Book crew who helped me envision this book long before it was ever written: Barbara, Kar, Emily, Lisa, Lara, Aimee, and Renee.

Want to give love to all the VelRo curators who have both encouraged and inspired me: Jenny, Dirk, Sofia. And a special shout out to the curators that I served with: Gavin, Presley and Lara.

Want to give love to the Nomadic Press editors who saw something in this work and who helped me shape it into something real: J. K., Michaela, Natasha, Paul, M.K. And to Grace Millard for the absolutely amazing cover illustration.

Want to give love to the many who have been really kind to me and who have inspired me in some type of way: Kayla, Nick, Logan, Gavin, Hannah, Austin, Loria, Paul, Brad, Keith, Jacob, Codi,

Kimberly, Heather, Philip, Danielle, Adam, Laura, Clem, Max, Clem, Margaret, Ruben, Aaron, Kacy, Matt, Jennifer, Jess, Amy, Simon, Nick, Evan, Teresa, Michael, Tongo, Jos, Steve, Kate, Andrew, Melissa, Joshua Jennifer, MK, Janine, Bob, James, John, Jen, Christine, Liam, Cassie, Manuel, Isobel, Arisa, Shawn, Vinnie.

If I somehow missed you, I'm sorry. Please know that I <3 you.

Based on the photograph by Kayla Eason.

Fisayo Adeyeye was born and raised in Southern California. He is the former Poetry Editor of *Fourteen Hills*, a co-curator of the VelRo Graduate Reading Series. His chapbook, *Blackfish*, was a finalist for the 2015 Best Prize Chapbook Contest (Big Lucks). He has works published in *Noble/Gas Qtrly*, *Nailed Magazine*, *New American Writing*, and *This Magazine*. You can talk to him about ants, whales, and other animals/objects of comparable size at fisayoadeyeye.com.